How Toys

Pulleys

Siân Smith

Heinemann
LIBRARY

Chicago, Illinois

www.capstonepub.com
Visit our website to find out more information about Heinemann-Raintree books.

To order:
☎ Phone 800-747-4992
🖳 Visit www.capstonepub.com to browse our catalog and order online.

Edited by Dan Nunn, Rebecca Rissman, and Sian Smith
Designed by Joanna Hinton-Malivoire
Picture research by Mica Brancic
Production by Victoria Fitzgerald

Originated by Capstone Global Library Ltd
Printed and bound in China by South China Printing Company Ltd

16 15 14 13 12
10 9 8 7 6 5 4 3 2 1

Library of Congress Cataloging-in-Publication Data
Smith, Siân.
    Pulleys / Siân Smith.
        p. cm.—(How toys work)
    Includes bibliographical references and index.
    ISBN 978-1-4329-6580-8 (hb)—ISBN 978-1-4329-6587-7 (pb)
    1. Pulleys—Juvenile literature. 2. Toys—Juvenile literature. I. Title.
    TJ1103.S65 2013
    621.8—dc23   2011041306

Acknowledgments
The author and publisher are grateful to the following for permission to reproduce copyright material: © Capstone Global Library Ltd pp.5, 6, 7, 8, 9, 11, 22b, 23 bottom (Karon Dubke), 12, 13, 14, 15, 18, 19, 20, 21, 23 top (Lord and Leverett), 16, 17 (Tudor Photography); Shutterstock pp.4 top left (© Galchenkova Ludmila), 4 bottom right (© Gorilla), 4 top right (© Hirurg), 4 bottom left (© Ron Zmiri), 10 (© Alberto Tirado), 22a (© Cheryl Casey), 22c (© bluecrayola), 22d (© Dikiiy).

Cover photograph of a boy on a zip line reproduced with permission of Corbis (© moodboard). Back cover photograph of a toy crane reproduced with permission of © Capstone Publishers (Karon Dubke).

We would like to thank David Harrison, Nancy Harris, Dee Reid, and Diana Bentley for their assistance in the preparation of this book.

Every effort has been made to contact copyright holders of material reproduced in this book. Any omissions will be rectified in subsequent printings if notice is given to the publisher.

All the Internet addresses (URLs) given in this book were valid at the time of going to press. However, due to the dynamic nature of the Internet, some addresses may have changed, or sites may have changed or ceased to exist since publication. While the author and publisher regret any inconvenience this may cause readers, no responsibility for any such changes can be accepted by either the author or the publisher.

Contents

Different Toys

There are many different kinds of toys.

Toys work in different ways.

Pulleys

pulley

Some toys use pulleys.

wheel

rope

A pulley is a wheel with a rope around it.

You can pull one end of the rope
to lift something up.

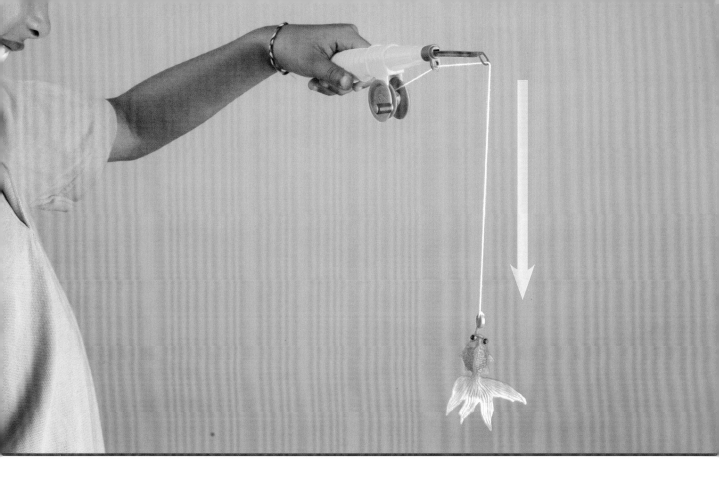

You can let go of the rope to move
something down.

pulley

A pulley can help us to lift heavy things.

A toy crane uses a pulley to
lift things.

Connecting Pulleys

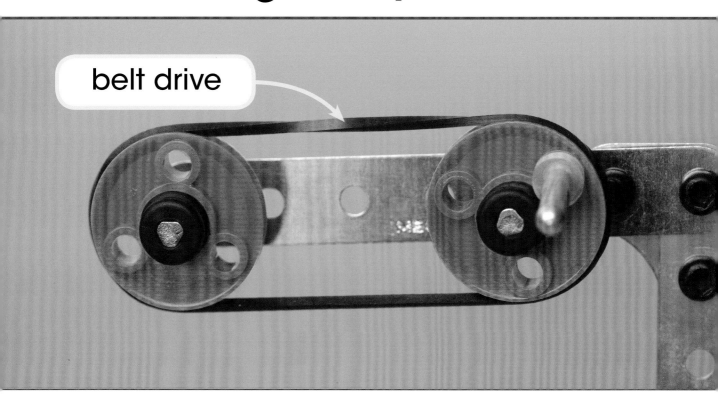

belt drive

You can connect two pulleys with a belt drive.

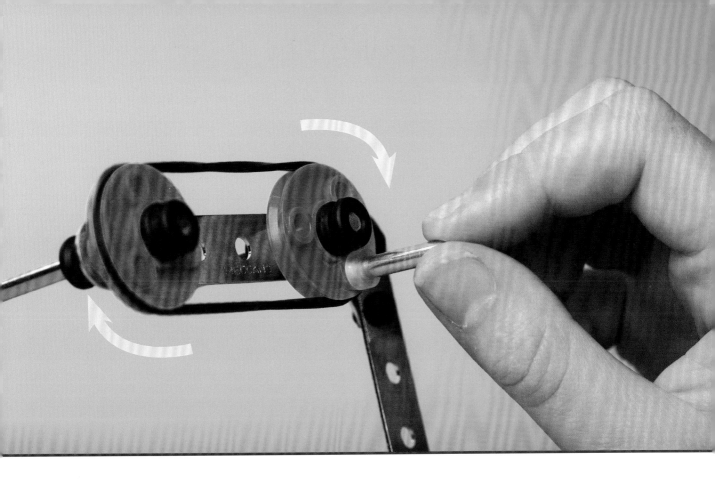

When you turn one pulley, the other one turns, too.

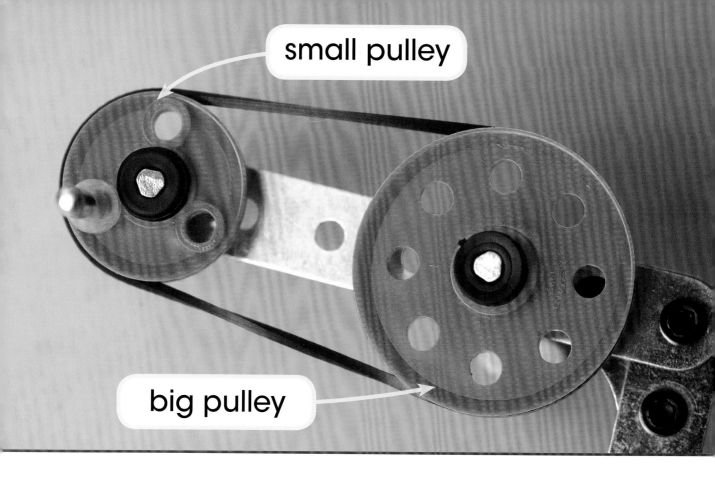

small pulley

big pulley

A big pulley and a small pulley can be joined together.

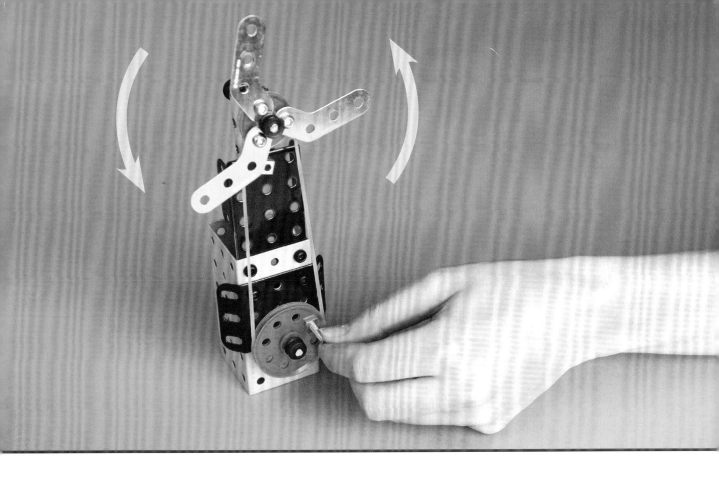

It is harder to push the big pulley.

But it makes the small pulley turn fast.

More Toys with Pulleys

pulley

This toy roller coaster works with a pulley.

The pulley takes the cars up to
the top.

pulley

This toy boat works with a pulley.

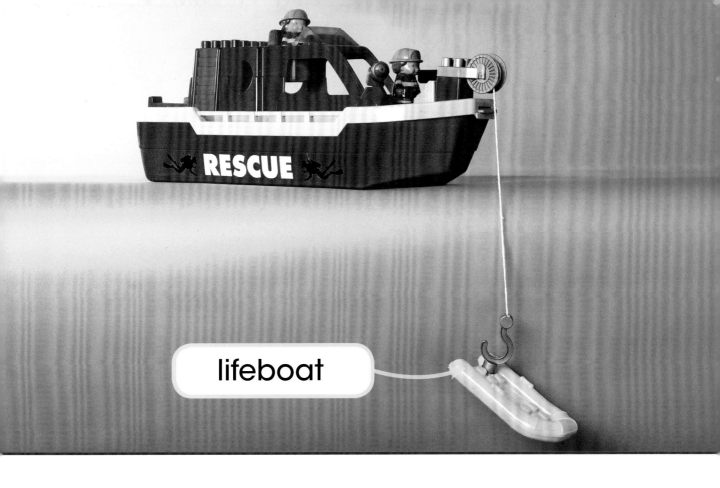

lifeboat

The pulley lifts lifeboats up
and down.

pulley

This toy truck works with a pulley.

The pulley lifts cars up and down.

Quiz

 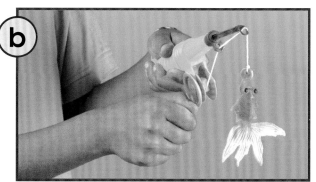

Which one of these toys uses a pulley to work?

Answer on page 24

Picture Glossary

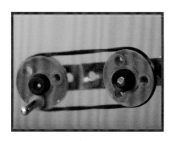 **belt drive** band that wraps around two wheels. It joins the wheels so that when one wheel turns, the other does, too.

 **pulley** wheel with a rope around it. We use pulleys to help us lift things up or put them down.

Index

Answer to question on page 22: Toy b uses a pulley to work.

Notes for Parents and Teachers

Introduction

Show the children a collection of toys. One or more of the toys should have a pulley mechanism. Ask the children if they can spot the toy with the pulley. Alternatively, show the children pictures of pulleys—for example, those used on a flagpole, a boat, and a crane. Do they know what a pulley is and what it does?

More information about pulleys

Explain that a pulley is a wheel with a rope, chain, or belt wrapped around it. Show the children an example of a grooved pulley wheel and explain that many pulleys have a dip or groove around the edge of the wheel, which stops the rope, chain, or belt from slipping off the sides. A pulley is a simple machine that helps us to lift things up or lower them down. Pulleys also make it easier for us to lift or move heavy things.

Follow-up activities

Support the children in using a construction set to create a working pulley. For example, you could make a simple crane and use this to lift something, or make a windmill similar to the one on page 15. For more advanced work on simple machines, children can work with an adult to discuss and play the games at: www.edheads.org/activities/simple-machines.